Mantra's English-Urdu
WORDS for School

Urdu Translation by Qamar Zamani

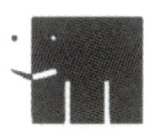

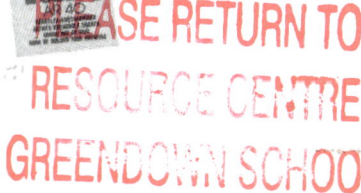

With special thanks to the teachers and children
of Moss Hall Infant and Junior Schools

Notes on Pronunciation
Please note that the transliterations in the book are
only a guide to how the words are pronounced.

Designed by Ian Heubner
Edited by Henriette Barkow

Text & Illustrations copyright © 1995 Mantra Publishing
First published in 1995 by Mantra Publishing Ltd
5 Alexandra Grove, London N12 8NU
http://www.mantrapublishing.com

English	Urdu	Transliteration
entrance hall	اندر داخل ہونے کا کمرہ	*under daakhil hone ka kumera*
classroom	کلاس روم	*classroom*
corridor	راہداری	*rahdari*
hall	بڑا کمرہ	*bera kumra*
office	دفتر	*dufter*
medical room	طبی امداد کا کمرہ	*lumbi rahdari*
staffroom	اساتذہ کا کمرہ	*asaataza ka kumra*
library	کتب خانہ	*kutub khana*
cloakroom	کوٹ ٹانگنے کی جگہ	*coat tangne ki jagah*

The School مدرسہ
Murdersa

3

English	Urdu	Transliteration
table	میز	*maiz*
chair	کرسی	*kursi*
desk	لکھنے کی ڈھلوان میز	*likhne ki dhalan maiz*
drawer	دراز	*daraaz*
chalk board	کھریا سے لکھنے کا تختہ	*khurya se likhne ka katakhta*
marker board	مارکر بورڈ	*marker board*
book case	کتابوں کی الماری	*kitabon ki alamari*
cupboard	الماری	*almari*
reading corner	پڑھنے کی جگہ	*pruhne ki jagah*
dressing up corner	کپڑے پہننے کی جگہ	*kupre pahnne ki jagah*
carpet	قالین	*qaaleen*
box	بکس	*bakas*
music	موسیقی	*mosiqi*

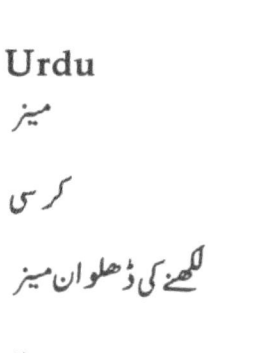

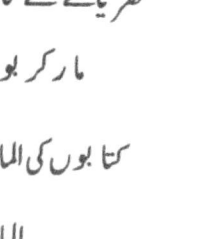
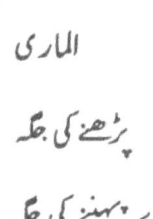
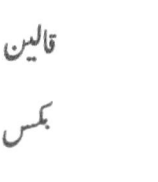
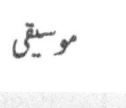

The Classroom
Classroom

کلاس روم

	English	Urdu	Transliteration
	toilets	غسل خانے یا بیت الخلا	*ghusal khana*
	toilet paper	غسل خانے میں استعمال کرنے کا کاغذ	*ghusal khane ka kaaghaz*
	paper towel	کاغذ کی تولیہ	*kaaghaz ki tauliya*
	towel	تولیہ	*tauliya*
	tissue/s	ٹشو یا پتلا کاغذ	*tissue/s*
	flush	فلش	*flush*

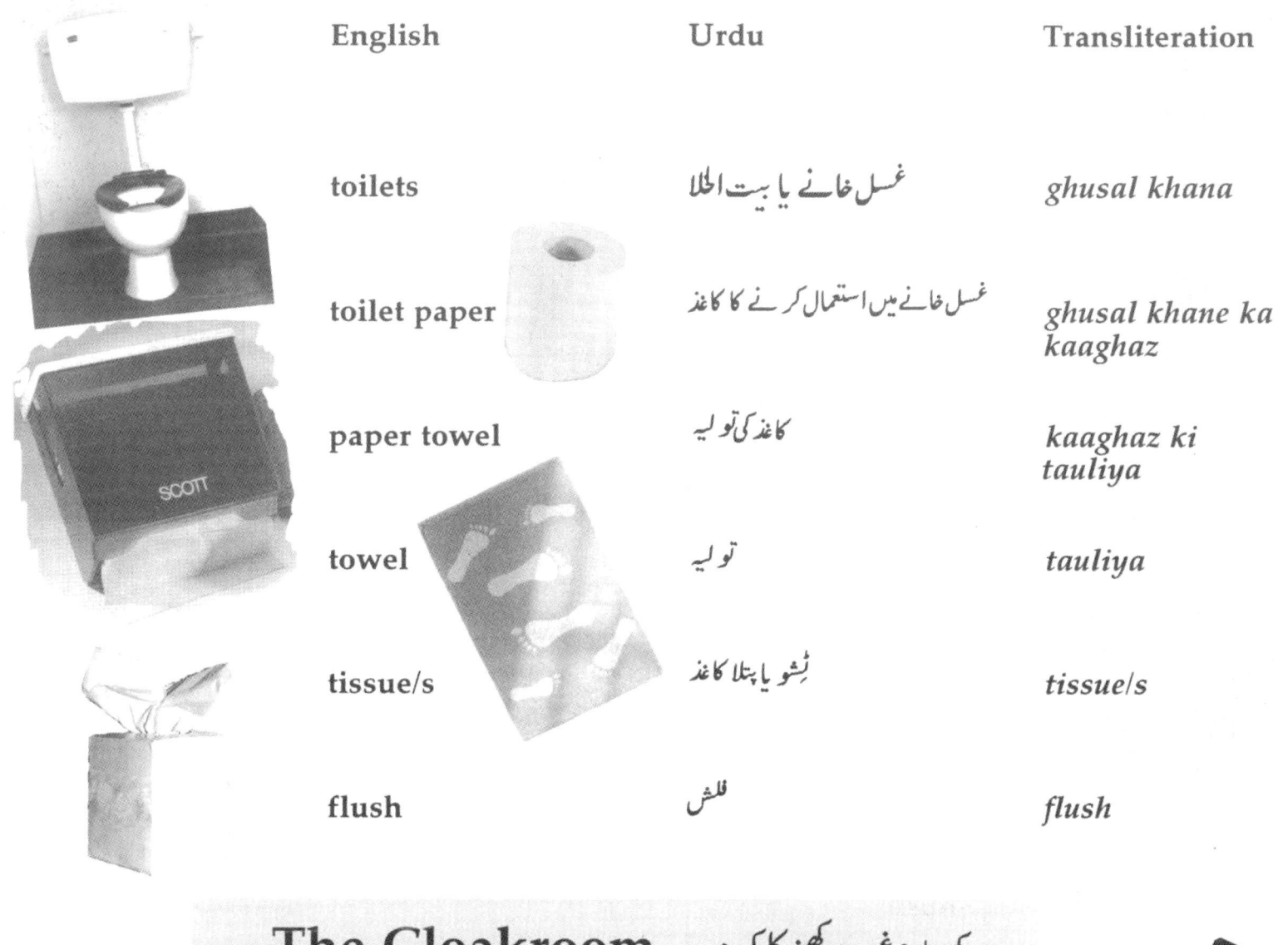

The Cloakroom کوٹ وغیرہ رکھنے کا کمرہ

Coat Rukhne Ka Kumra

5

English	Urdu	Transliteration
peg	کھونٹی	khoonti
sink	برتن دھونے کی جگہ	berten dhone ki jegha
plug	پلگ	plug
water	پانی	paani
soap	صابن	saaban
hand dryer	ہاتھ سکھانے کا آلہ	haatha sukhana ka aala
cubicle	چھوٹا کمرہ یا جگہ	chota kumra
wet	گیلا	geela
dry	سوکھا	sookha

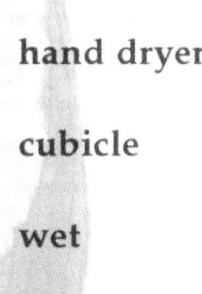

6

The Cloakroom کوٹ وغیرہ رکھنے کا کمرہ
Coat Rukhne Ka Kumra

English	Urdu	Transliteration
playground	کھیل کامیدان	*khel ka maidan*
climbing frame	چڑھنے کاچوکھٹا	*churhne ka chaukhta*
slide	پھسلنے کی سیڑھی	*phisalne ki seerhi*

English	Urdu	Transliteration
bench	بینچ	*bench*
wall	دیوار	*deewar*

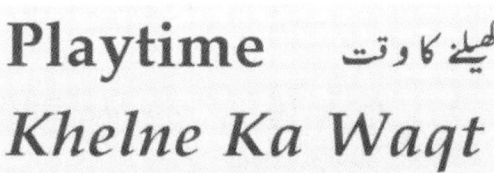

Playtime کھیلنے کا وقت
Khelne Ka Waqt

۷

8

English	Urdu	Transliteration
ball	گیند	*gaind*
game	کھیل	*khel*
whistle	سیٹی	*seeti*
bell	گھنٹی	*ghunti*
gate	پھاٹک	*phatak*
skipping rope	کودنے کی رسی	*koodne ki russi*

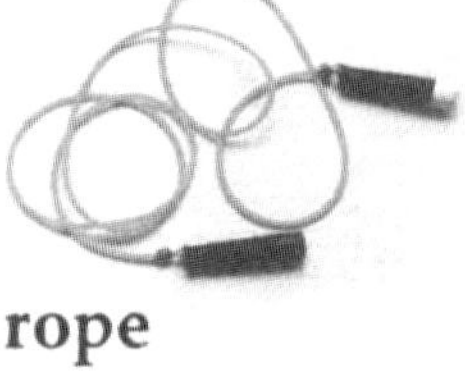

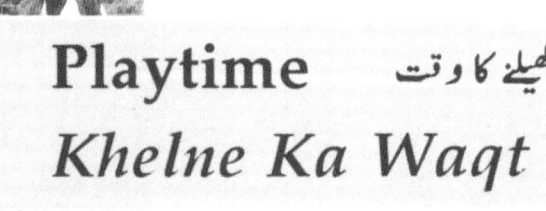

Playtime کھیلنے کا وقت
Khelne Ka Waqt

English	Urdu	Transliteration
school dinners	اسکول کا کھانا	school ka khana
packed lunch	پیک کیا ہوا کھانا	pack kiya hua khana
flask	فلاسک	flask
lunch box	کھانا رکھنے کا ڈبہ	khana rakhne ka dibba

9

English	Urdu	Transliteration
spoon	چمچہ	chumcha
knife	چاقو	chaaqu
fork	کانٹا	kaanta
plate	پلیٹ	plate

Lunch دوپہر کا کھانا
Dopeher Ka Khana

10

English	Urdu	Transliteration
cup/mug/beaker	پیالی ، مگ ، بیکر	*pyali mug*
food	کھانا	*khana*
eat	کھانا	*khana*
drink	مشروب	*mushroob*
queue	قطار	*qutaar*
too little/not enough	بہت کم ، ناکافی	*bohet kum*
more	اورزیادہ	*aur ziada*
too much	بہت زیادہ	*bohet ziada*
finish	ختم ، خاتمہ	*khutam*

Lunch دوپہر کا کھانا
Dopeher Ka Khana

English		Urdu	Transliteration
	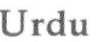		
boy		لڑکا	*lurka*
girl		لڑکی	*lurki*
child		بچہ	*bachcha*

11

English	Urdu	Transliteration
teacher/head	نگراں استاد یا استانی	*nigraan ustaad*
teacher	استاد ، استانی	*ustaad/ustaani*
welfare assistant	دیکھ بھال کرنے والے لوگ	*dikh bhaal-kernewale loag*
mealtime supervisor	کھانے کے وقت کے نگراں	*khane ke waqt kir nigram*
secretary	سیکریٹری	*secretary*
cook	باورچی	*baavarchi*

draw a picture and stick it here

The People
Loag

لوگ

English	Urdu	Transliteration
parent	والدین	*valdain*
father	باپ , والد	*baap*
you	آپ , تم	*aap, tum*
me	میں	*main*
brother	بھائی	*bhai*
sister	بہن	*behen*
mother	ماں , والدہ	*maa*
friend	دوست	*doast*
neighbour	پڑوسی	*purosi*

12

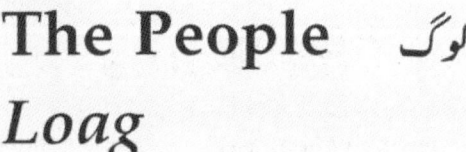

draw a picture and stick it here

The People لوگ
Loag

English	Urdu	Transliteration
book	کتاب	*kitaab*
writing book	لکھنے کی کتاب	*likhne ki kitaab*
reading book	پڑھنے کی کتاب	*purhne ki kitaab*
maths/number book	حساب کی کتاب	*hisaab ki kitaab*
newspaper	اخبار	*akhbar*

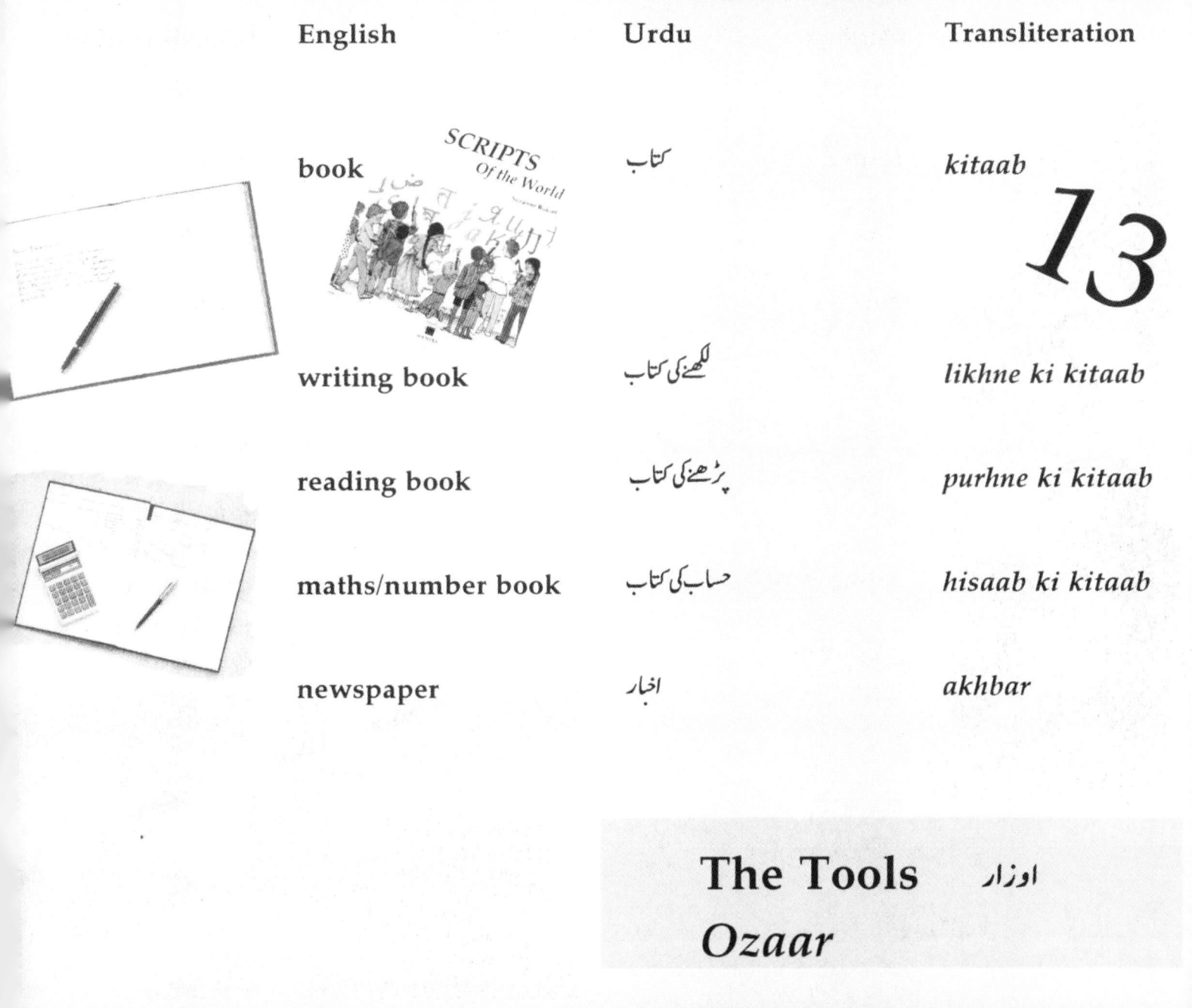

13

The Tools اوزار

Ozaar

English	Urdu	Transliteration
pencil	پنسل	pencil
pencil sharpener	پنسل شارپنر	pencil sharpener
pencil case	پنسل رکھنے کا تھیلا	pencil rukhne ka thaila
crayon	رنگنے والی کھریا	rungne wali
felt tip pen	فیلٹ والا قلم	felt wala qalam kharya
ruler	رُولر	ruler
rubber	ربر	rubber

The Tools   اوزار
Ozaar

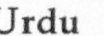

English	Urdu	Transliteration
scissors	قينچی	qainchi
glue	گوند	goand
sticky tape	چپکنے والا ٹیپ	chupakne wala tape
paper	کاغذ	kaaghaz
paint	رنگ	rung
paintbrush	رنگنے کا برش	rungne ka brush
computer	کمپیوٹر	computer
screen	سکرین	screen
keyboard	کی بورڈ	keyboard
mat	چٹائی ـ میٹ	chatai
mouse	ماؤس	mouse

The Tools
Ozaar

اوزار

15

English		Urdu	Transliteration

16

English	Urdu	Transliteration
tape recorder	ٹیپ ریکارڈر	*tape recorder*
cassette/tape	کیسٹ ـ ٹیپ	*cassette/tape*

television	ٹیلی ویژن	*television*
video	ویڈیو	*video*

telephone	ٹیلی فون	*telephone*
folder/file	فولڈر / فائل	*file*
counters	گنتی کرنے کے اوزار	*ginti kurne ke ozaar*
money	روپیہ ، ریز گاری	*rupee*

The Tools   اوزار
Ozaar

English	Urdu	Transliteration
sweatshirt	سوٹ شرٹ	*sweatshirt*
jumper	جمپر	*jumper*
tights	ٹائٹس	*tights*
t shirt	ٹی شرٹ	*t shirt*

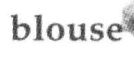

English	Urdu	Transliteration
blouse	بلاوَز	*blouse*
cardigan	سویٹر، کارڈیگن	*sweater*
dress	لباس	*dress*
skirt	سکرٹ	*skirt*

The Clothes کپڑے، لباس
Kupre, Libaas

17

English	Urdu	Transliteration
trousers	پتلون	*putloon*
shorts	شورٹس	*shorts*
knickers	جانگیہ	*jangiya*
shirt	قمیص	*qamees*
tie	نکٹائی	*neck tie*
blazer	بلیزر	*blazer*
socks	موزے	*moze*
shoe/s	جوتے	*joote*
plimsolls	ربرکےجوتے	*rubber ke joote*

18 The Clothes كپڑے، لباس
Kupre, Libaas

English	Urdu	Transliteration
coat	کوٹ	*coat*
jacket	جیکٹ	*jacket*
hat	ٹوپی	*toupi*
gloves	دستانے	*dustaane*
overall	اوپر پہننے کی پوشاک	*ooper pahn-ne ki poshak*
apron	بالا پوش	*baala posh*
swimming costume	تیرنے کا لباس	*tairne ka libaas*
swimming hat/cap	تیرنے کی ٹوپی	*tairne ki topi*

19

The Clothes کپڑے، لباس
Kupre, Libaas

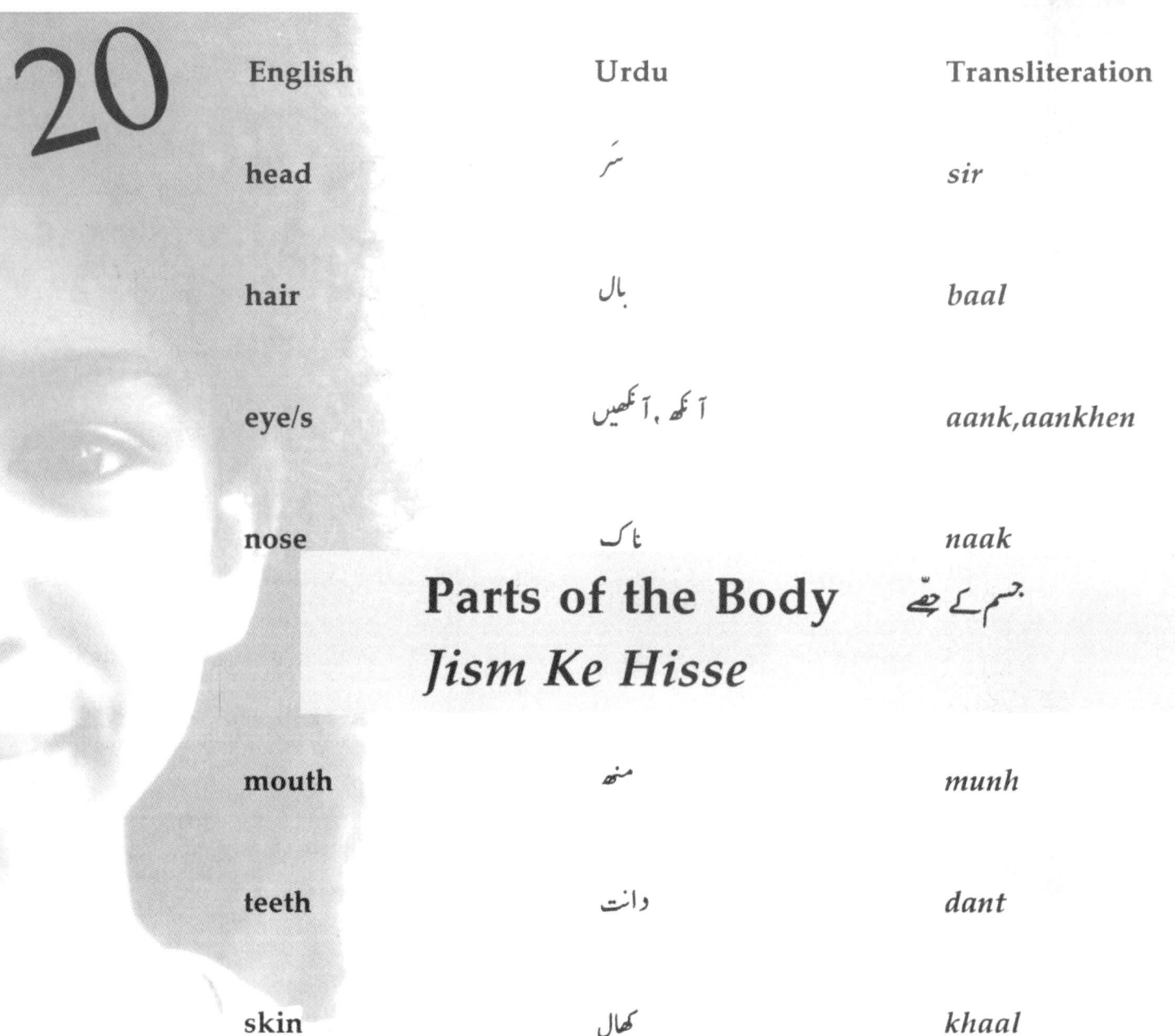

English	Urdu	Transliteration
head	سَر	*sir*
hair	بال	*baal*
eye/s	آنکھ، آنکھیں	*aank, aankhen*
nose	ناک	*naak*

Parts of the Body جسم کے حصّے
Jism Ke Hisse

English	Urdu	Transliteration
mouth	منہ	*munh*
teeth	دانت	*dant*
skin	کھال	*khaal*

English	Urdu	Transliteration
hand	ہاتھ	haath
thumb	انگوٹھا	ungootha
finger	انگلی	ungli
arm	بازو	baazu
elbow	کہنی	kohni

Parts of the Body جسم کے حصے
Jism Ke Hisse

21

leg/s	ٹانگ ، ٹانگیں	taang, tangen
knee	گھٹنا	ghutna
foot	پیر	paer
toe	پیر کی انگلی	paer ki ungli

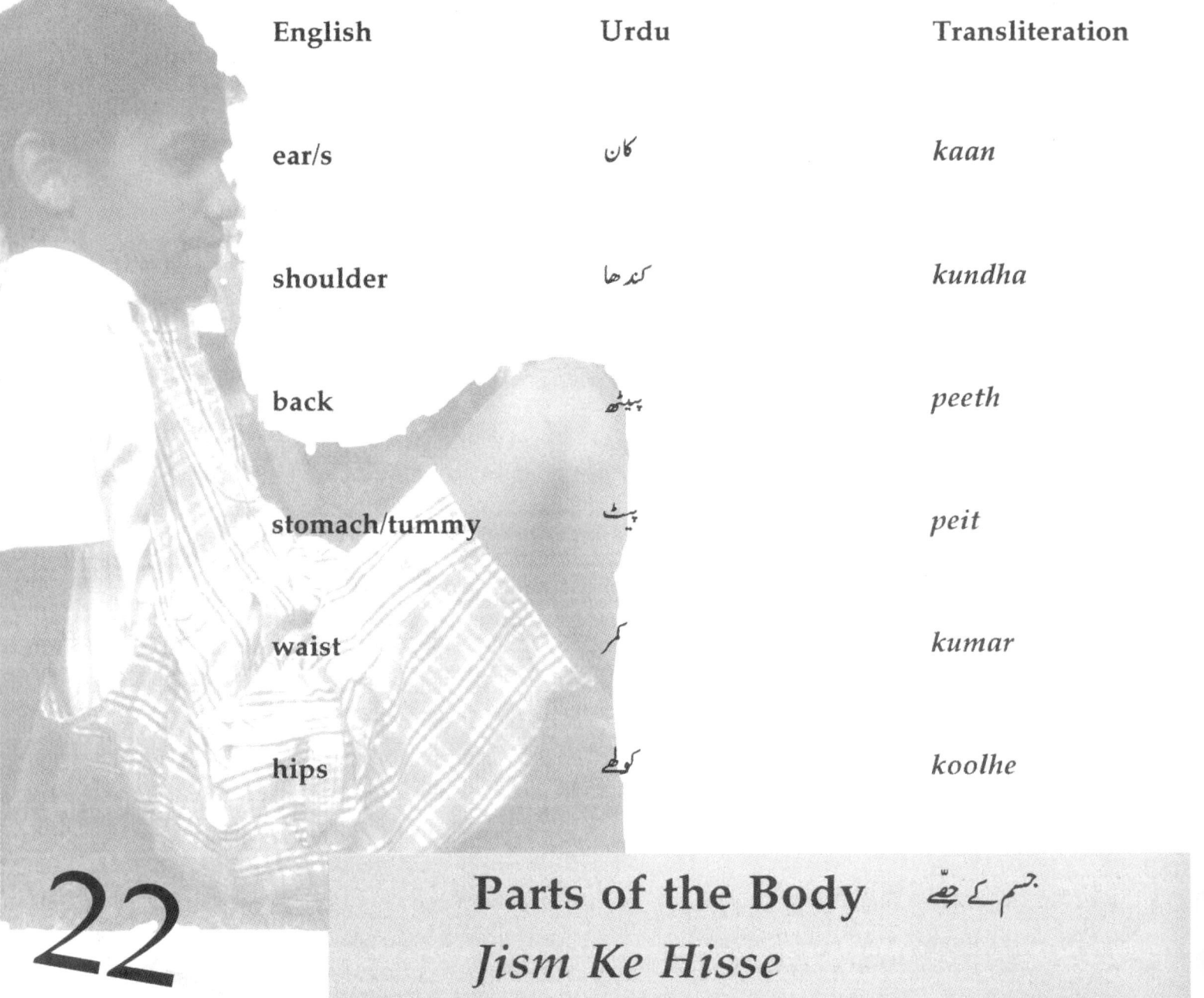

English	Urdu	Transliteration
ear/s	کان	*kaan*
shoulder	کندھا	*kundha*
back	پیٹھ	*peeth*
stomach/tummy	پیٹ	*peit*
waist	کمر	*kumar*
hips	کولھے	*koolhe*

22 Parts of the Body جسم کے حصے
Jism Ke Hisse

English	Urdu	Transliteration
yes	جی ہاں	*jee haan*
no	جی نہیں	*jee nahin*
now	ابھی	*abhi*
today	آج	*aaj*
holiday	چھٹیاں	*chuttiyan*
birthday	سالگرہ	*saalgirah*
look	دیکھو	*dekho*
again	پھر یا دوبارہ	*phir ya dobaara*
listen	سُنو	*suno*
draw	تصویر بنانا	*tasvir banana*
copy	نقل یا نقل کرنا	*naqal*
write	لکھنا	*likhna*
choose	منتخب کرنا	*muntakhib karna*
read	پڑھنا	*purhna*
like	پسند کرنا	*pasand karna*
dislike	ناپسند کرنا	*na pasand karna*
hot	گرم	*garam*
cold	ٹھنڈا	*thanda*

Other Useful Words
کچھ اور کارآمد الفاظ
Kuch Aur Karamad Ulfaz

23

INDEX